## *HOW TO DO IT!*

No matter what it is, the important question always is: "How to do it?"

The mind has many marvelous powers—far more than you have ever dreamed of—and humanity has barely begun the wonderful evolutionary journey that will let us tap into them all at will. We grow in our abilities as we do things.

There are many wonderful things you can do. As you do them, you learn more about the innate qualities of mind and spirit, and as exercise these inner abilities, they will grow in strength—*as will your vision of your mental and spiritual potential.*

In making a *Love Charm*, or using a *Magic Mirror*, or *Dreaming Lucky Lotto Numbers*, or many other strange and wonderful things, you are extending—just a little bit—the tremendous gift that lies within, the Life Force itself.

We are born that we may grow, and not to use this gift—not to grow in your perception and understanding of it—is to turn away from the gifts of Life, of Love, of Beauty, of Happiness that are the very reason for Creation.

Learning how to do these things is to open psychic windows to New Worlds of Mind & Spirit. Actually doing these things is to enter into New Worlds. Each of these things that we do is a step forward in accepting responsibility for the worlds that you can shape and influence.

Simple, easy to follow, yet so very rewarding. Following these step-by-step instructions can start you upon high adventure. Gain control over the world around you, and step into *New Worlds of Mind & Spirit.*

## About the Author

Tara Buckland is a long-time student and practitioner of the ancient wisdoms. From a formal education in comparative religions, she progressed over the years to research and involvement in many branches of her earlier studies, always keeping a special interest in, and attunement to, the religion and magickal practices of the Ancient Egyptians. She is a Priestess of Isis and a long-time Priestess and leader of Wicca. Married to well-known author Raymond Buckland, Tara has had ample opportunity to observe and participate in religious and magickal rituals of many types.

Born and raised in Ohio, Tara lived in Scotland for a year attending the University of Edinburgh. She studied music all her life and plays the violin, piano, guitar, pennywhistle, bodhran and synthesizer, composing many songs for the Pagan community.

## To Write to the Author

We cannot guarantee that every letter written to the author can be answered, but all will be forwarded. Both the author and the publisher appreciate hearing from readers, learning of your enjoyment and benefit from this book. Llewellyn publishes a bimonthly news magazine with news and reviews of practical esoteric studies and articles helpful to the student, and some readers' questions and comments may be answered through this magazine's columns if permission to do so is included in the original letter. The author sometimes participates in seminars and workshops, and dates and places are announced in the *Llewellyn New Times*. To write to the author, or to ask a question, write to:

Tara Buckland
c/o The Llewellyn New Times
P.O. Box 64383-087, St. Paul, MN 55164-0383, U.S.A.

Please enclose a self-addressed, stamped envelope for reply, or $1.00 to cover costs.

# How To Make an Easy Charm to Attract Love Into Your Life

## Tara Buckland

1990
Llewellyn Publications
P.O. Box 64383, St. Paul, MN 55164-0383, U.S.A.

International Standard Book Number: 0-87542-087-7
Library of Congress Catalog Number: 90-6018

First Edition, 1990
First Printing, 1990

Cover Design: Christopher Wells

Produced by Llewellyn Publications
Typography and Art Property of Llewellyn Worldwide, Ltd.

Published by
LLEWELLYN PUBLICATIONS
A Division of Llewellyn Worldwide, Ltd.
P.O. Box 64383
St. Paul, MN 55164-0383, U.S.A.

Printed in the United States of America

# Other How To Books From Llewellyn

*How to Make and Use a Magic Mirror*
    by Donald Tyson

*How to Dream Your Lucky Lotto Numbers*
    by Ralph Maltagliati

# Contents

*Part I*

# Chapter 1

## *Egypt and Isis*

### The Land of Magick

The civilization of the ancient Egyptians was one of the greatest the world has ever known. It spanned over 3000 years, from about 3100 B.C.E. ("Before Common Era" is a more generally accepted term than "Before Christ") to about 30 B.C.E. If we compare the length of the civilization of Egypt with those of Greece and Rome, we find that the ancient Egyptian culture lasted four times longer than the magnificent Greek civilization and more than three times as long as the mighty Roman empire.

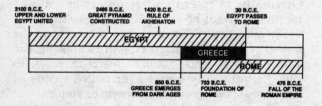

Throughout the ages, Egypt has been considered the cradle of magick, and rightly so, for the Egyptians had one of the most highly developed magickal systems the world has ever known. By the fourth dynasty (about 2500 B.C.E.), ancient papyrus writings show that magick was clearly established as a recognized art, although it must have had its foundations much earlier than that— probably in Neolithic times.

Egyptian magick relied primarily on the use of amulets, charms, magickal figures, pictures and formulas/chants. The Egyptians used magick as a cure for a great variety of problems: for protection from storms, wild animals, illness, wounds, poisons, and even ghosts.

Of the various types of magick used, amulets and charms were the most popular. An amulet is an object which is created specifically for a magickal purpose. It usually has some meaningful shape, or inscription, and bestows magickal power on the person who uses it. In Egypt, amulets were awakened by "charming."

A charm is really a magickal formula, chant, spell or words of power applied to a person, place or thing. "To charm" is to put a spell on something. Originally, to refer to a person as "charming" meant that she or he was spellbinding or supernaturally attractive. Often the word is applied to the object which was charmed—thus making the words "charm" and "amulet" interchangeable. To put it simply, any object over which words of power are spoken becomes a charm or amulet.

The Egyptians had amulets and charms for everything. Many of these, such as the ankh and the scarab, became very well known and have remained powerful symbols down through the centuries even into our own culture. On the following pages are tables of some of the more popular Egyptian amulets.

# Amulets

*Utchat.*
Right Eye of Ra, The Sun (Protection)

*Utchat.*
Left Eye of Ra. The Moon (Protection)

*Aat.*
The Backbone (Strength)

*Kheper.*
Scarab (Prosperity, Life, Becoming)

## Amulets

Lotus flower of Isis
(Transformation,
Growth)

*Ra.*
The Sun God
(Life, Strength, Health)

Sun's Disk with Uraei
(Power, Dominion)

Winged Disk (Rebirth, Eternal Life)

# Amulets

*Tchetch.*
Tree Trunk That
Held the Dead
Body of Osiris
(Stability, Strength)

Ankh, Male/Female
Symbol of Union (Life)

*Thet.*
Knot of Isis—A Pop-
ular Representation of
the Power of Knot
Magick (Power, New
Life To Hold Together,
Protection of Isis)

*Auset.*
Throne of Isis (Power of
Isis)

In addition to the extensive use of charms and amulets, the Egyptians made great use of astrological tables and numerology. Egypt is credited by the Greeks as being the birthplace of astrology and numerology. Numbers were sacred to the Egyptians, and they included numbers in all their magickal formulas, as will be dealt with later. The pyramids are perhaps the greatest example where numerology was used to create a magickal effect.

*Isis, Lady of Ten Thousand Names*

Out of the deep and mysterious depths of the religion of the ancient Egyptians a single deity arose to surpass all the others. Her name is Isis and She has been continuously worshipped from the dawn of Egyptian culture through to the present day—for over 5,000 years.

The story of Isis is the oldest of the Savior God/Goddess legends. In this story Isis and Osiris reigned as Pharaoh and Queen over the great land of Egypt. Their brother, Set, was jealous of the Pharaoh's fame and wealth and plotted his death.

Set threw a great party in honor of his brother,

Osiris. At this party he proudly displayed a magnificent coffin which was inlaid with gold, silver and precious jewels.

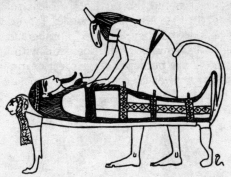

Here, truly, was a coffin to honor the Gods and to bring certain glory to whomever was buried in it! Set held a contest for the coffin. Each person at the party was to lay down in it, and the person who fit it exactly would win it as a prize. The Pharaoh, Osiris, was the first to try it out. Alas, the coffin was a trap, and no sooner had the mighty Pharaoh laid down than the top was put on and quickly nailed shut. The coffin was thrown into the Nile and the currents carried it out to sea.

Queen Isis was stricken with grief over her lost husband. She was said to have traveled to many foreign lands in search of the jeweled coffin. Finally, after many years, Isis came upon the shores of Phoenicia where Queen Astarte, pitying but not recognizing the Goddess, hired her as nursemaid to the infant Prince. Isis took good care of the boy and began working on a spell of immortality on the infant, a spell which involved placing the Prince in a smoldering fire. Unfortunately, Queen

Astarte saw the child in the fire and grabbed him out, thereby breaking the spell and forever robbing him of that gift.

When Isis was called before the council to account for her actions, her true identity was revealed. Queen Astarte was able to help her retrieve Osiris by revealing that a beautiful tamarisk tree near the shores of the ocean had been discovered which had apparently grown up around a jeweled coffin. The tree was so magnificent that it had been cut down, left whole, and used as a pillar in the palace temple. Little did the Phoenicians realize that the body of the great King Osiris was contained within the fragrant, jeweled tamarisk tree.

Isis carried the tree-sheltered corpse back to Egypt. The evil Set heard of their return and managed, once again, to get his hands on the body of the Pharaoh. This time, he chopped the body up into little bits before throwing it into the Nile. Isis had to search, not just for one piece, but many. She managed to find all the parts except one, the penis. In substitution she created a gold penis and put her husband back together again. With her secrets of embalming (Isis was said to have created the art of embalming) and her magickal words, her husband was resurrected and is said to return each year with the corn harvest.

Isis was the supreme Goddess of Magick, and because of Her unfailing love of Osiris she became the Great Goddess of Love and Healing. She had healing shrines all over Egypt, Greece and Rome, and great cures were attributed to Her powers. She was a solace to Kings and peasants alike, and because Isis was all things to all people, in later years She became a very great rival of the fledgling Christian faith.

> "There, in the beginning was Isis. Oldest of the old, She was the Goddess from Whom all Becoming arose. She was the Great Lady-Mistress of the Two Lands of Egypt, Mistress of Shelter, Mistress of Heaven, Mistress of the House of Life, Mistress of the Word of God. She was the Unique. In all Her great and wonderful works She was a wiser magician and more excellent than any other God."
>
> —Müller, D.

Isis promised Her devoted followers: "You shall live in blessing, you shall live glorious in my protection; and when you have fulfilled your allotted span of life and descend to the underworld, there too you shall see me, as you see me now, shining...And if you show yourself obedient to My divinity...you will know that I alone have permitted you to extend your life beyond the time allocated you by your destiny."

The fame and worship of Isis spread to other lands and She was adopted into the Greek and then the Roman pantheons. When Her worship spread to Rome, Her power, fame and devotion spread like wildfire to every corner of the Roman Empire. Her priests were dedicated missionaries, and the Egyptian faith became a dominant force in Italy. In Rome, Pompeii and other Italian cities, temples and obelisks were erected in Her honor and the great Emperors bowed to Her name.

She took possession of the traditional hallowed centers of Greek worship—Delos, Delphi, Eleusis and Athens. Temples were erected to Her on the shores of the Arabian Gulf and the Black Sea. She had faithful followers in Gaula and Spain, in Pannonia and Germany. Her worship held sway from Arabia and Asia Minor in the east to Portugal and Britain in the west. Shrines were erected to Her in cities large and small: Beneventum, the Piraeus and London. She became known as the Lady of Ten Thousand Names because in every country She went to She absorbed many of the identities and attributes of the local Goddesses.

The Isian religion was the greatest religion of the Western World prior to the advent of Christianity. Although Her religion eventually lost political power to the zealous missionaries of Christianity, Her worship was never entirely obliterated. During the time when the Holy Roman Church was persecuting all non-Christians, Her Priests and Priestesses went " underground" with their religion. Down through the centuries there have remained secret pockets of Her worshippers

who have kept Her love and teachings alive. These underground temples became known as secret societies and are still active today. It is from these people, and the many written records left by the Egyptians, that we can glean many of the old magickal techniques that were used in ancient Egypt.

The Christians eventually incorporated much from the Isian religion into their own religion in order to help persuade people to accept the new faith. The Virgin Mary with her blue mantle is taken directly from images of Isis, as are many of her titles: "The Maiden," "She Whose Praises Are Innumerable," "The Great First Principle," "She Who Initiates," and so on.

Much of the ceremonial side of Christianity was also taken from the ceremonies of Isis. The black cassock with the white surplus was worn by the Priests of Isis, much as it is today by the Christian priests. Aspects such as penance, fasting, confession, holy water, etc., were also taken directly from Isian Mysteries. The Church tore down the temples to Isis and reused those same stones to construct its own churches, so that the local people would feel familiarity in going to the same spot for worship.

# Chapter 2

# *Magick*

## What Is Magick?

Magick is the ability to make things happen in accordance with your own desires. It is not the same as "stage magic," where tricks are performed for people's amazement by gadgets and "sleight-of-hand" movements. Stage magic imitates the concepts behind real magick, but accomplishes this by deception rather than by reality. To distinguish between the two types of magick we have spelled the older, genuine tradition of magick with a "k" on the end of the word.

Although wands are sometimes used in real magick, the image of a great wizard or fairy godmother waving a wand and "poof!" an object appears out of "thin air" is somewhat exaggerated. Nevertheless, magick does appear to be mysterious and supernatural to those who do not understand it.

Actually, magick is something that is quite natural to humankind and has been a part of our scene since the first human stood upright on two legs. Even in this modern age, magick—the discussion, romance and practice of it—still exists.

Working magick is making use of powers that are natural to the human body. Modern anthropologists see the "primitive" belief in magick as being based on superstitious fears of people who cannot comprehend the world around them. It is true to say that what we do not know or understand is often mysterious and fearsome. Primitive people attempted to appease the unknown by making use of the only tool they possessed—their own natural power.

The naïveté here is on the part of the "modern" scientist who automatically attributes such practices to ignorance. Why do we automatically discount such natural practices? Magick is absolutely universal in "primitive" cultures. Could this be because it is something that is natural to the human animal—as natural as hibernation is to the bear?

*The Barley Dance*

Absolutely yes! Magick is making use of that power that all humans possess. Humans who live closer to nature, such as many of the so-called "primitive" cultures, instinctively feel this power. When cultures who have been separated from their natural roots meet those who still practice magick, they either dismiss it as superstitious nonsense or they become frightened of it and label it as "evil" and as "consorting with demons."

Another aspect of magick that is universally found throughout the world and throughout all cultures is the fact that children automatically believe in it. This is because they have not yet been taught to distrust their natural instincts. It is not that they are stupid, but that they are unpolluted by cultural beliefs and social values.

## Words of Power

Modern day metaphysicians (the New Age term for "magicians") have identified this natural power in a simple phrase: "As you believe, so you achieve." Words and thoughts are things. They are alive in the sense that it is believed that all physical life can be reduced to a word or a thought. If you think certain thoughts and say certain words in just the right way, then you will manifest your desire into the physical world.

As stated in the previous chapter, an amulet or charm is some object over which "words of power" are spoken. What exactly are "words of power"? Are they some mysterious mumbo-jumbo spoken in an ancient language that has been used for 10,000 years? They can be, though they do not have to be so, and that is not why they are "words of power."

To speak from the diaphragm (from the abdomen) in a tone of voice that *will be obeyed*— this is where the "voice of power" emanates. We have all heard people use the "voice of power" from time to time. An example that most people can remember is the parent or teacher who has become really exasperated with us and uses that tone of voice which you *know* means business!

To use the "voice of power" on any words makes them "words of power." It's as simple as that.

Magicians feel that people are constantly creating the world around them by the continuous thoughts that go on in their heads. Magick is simply using thoughts and words deliberately to create the desired effect. The noisemaking and ceremony that often accompanies magickal rituals are simply techniques to access deeper states of mind (which is often known as "ecstasy"). This state can be reached by many different techniques: dance, prayer, meditation, repetitious chants, hypnosis, or even singing.

This ecstatic state is always an emotional experience, even if you're using quiet meditation to achieve it. Therefore, it is safe to say that effective magick is always an emotional experience. (Mr. Spock and his fellow Vulcans would have been lousy magicians!)

## White Magick—Black Magick

"What you think about, you bring about." Magick, an innate power in all humans, is closely related to the power of thoughts. Words, and the ability to speak (an extension of thinking) is often overlooked as the tremendous power source that it is. Your words have the power to hurt others; you can ruin a marriage, cause the loss of a job, create strife and war, and even influence death.

Does this mean that words and the ability to

speak are evil? Of course not, for we all know that speech is also able to become poetry, inspire confidence, express love and appreciation, promote peace, verbalize devotion, heal and even occasionally prevent death.

Those who fear magick often do so because they believe it to come from some mysterious source—maybe even from a "devil." Learning to understand your own energy and relationship to the universe is all the mystery to be revealed here. Obviously, as with the power of the spoken word, the natural energy of magick can be used in a positive or negative manner. How much impact can we really have on others, and why is it important to avoid negative or "black" magick?

Black magick is using this natural magickal power in such a way as to deliberately cause disharmony, destruction, deterioration, disruption or death. Forcing the will of another to do your bidding falls under disruption, and is very definitely black magick.

**Personal Power**

One of the great metaphysical laws is actually a contradiction:

> Everything we do, think, and say, has a profound impact upon every thing and every person in this universe. Yet it is also true that nothing comes to you that you do not allow to enter your life (either deliberately or by confusion, ignorance or neglect).

How can this be? Magicians see God/Goddess as manifest in all things: people, stones, plants and even the wind. This means that when God/Goddess created life, He/She also *became* life. We are all tiny aspects of God/Goddess/All-That-Is, and if we listen closely to the voice within us, we can hear the guidance of that Spark of the Divine. We are all one, yet separate. As creators we have complete control over our lives and a shared control over the Universe. As the created, we are receptive to the influence of others, hence the apparent contradiction.

To grow in power magickally means to take more and more responsibility for the Creator aspect of ourselves. To be responsible for the growth and well-being not only of ourselves but also of other people, of animals, plants and the very earth we live on. A powerful magician can influence world politics and shape our world in fantastic ways.

Taking responsibility is achieved through self-knowledge and self-love. As a magician becomes more powerful, negative energies or situations can more easily be neutralized. Getting back to the example with words, the more a person knows, trusts, and loves her/himself, the less likely it is that evil gossip will disrupt her/his life.

Most magicians and metaphysicians of today believe in reincarnation. Reincarnation is the idea that we live more than one life, ever evolving into a wiser person. It is also believed that each person creates her/his own destiny and is ultimately responsible for it. This means that no one else makes your choices for you. Only *you* can choose your path, and sooner or later everyone moves toward the light.

As with slanderous gossip, a magician practicing negative magick may certainly be able to influence another person. Sooner or later, however, that person will recover—if not in this lifetime, then in some other one—and will be back on his/her path to the light. At worst the effect is temporary.

### The Law of Threefold Return

This is the most important law of the universe. It states that whatever you give out returns to you threefold. Where is the inducement to do negative magick? If you were to send out manipulative, controlling energy, that is what you would receive back, multiplied by three! If you send out positive thoughts and love, this will return to you threefold.

## Love Magick

In magick—especially love magick—it is always safest to work on yourself rather than someone else. In other words, if you want to bring love into your life, work the magick on yourself. Make yourself attractive to others and work in generalities by specifying that the right person will come to you. If you feel a strong attraction toward a particular person, then do magick to bring a person with those particular characteristics to you. Make a list of what you like about that person—the color of hair, interests, physique, age, etc.—and work to bring someone similar to you. If this person happens to be right, then she/he will come; if not, then someone else *who is just right for you* will come instead.

Suppose Jane Smith is tremendously attracted to Jason Brown, the local heart-throb of all the girls. She loves his rugged good looks, his blond hair, etc. But instead of aiming her magick at Jason Brown she makes a list of what she really likes about him and works her magick to bring someone with those characteristics to her.

If you do magick to try to bring a *specific* person to you—no matter how pure your intentions —*you are dealing in black magick for you are interfering with that person's free will.*

## How Does Magick Work?

The magickal power that all humans possess is a dynamic combination of the power of words combined with imagination, emotion and intent. Magickal ceremonies are constructed in such a way as to arouse the emotion of the magician and to provide structure to achieve the union of these different aspects.

As stated earlier, magicians work with the Threefold Law of the Universe: *Whatever you send out returns to you threefold!* A thought returns threefold for a thought, a word returns threefold for a word, an emotion returns threefold for an emotion, and an action returns threefold for an action. Here is where magick differs somewhat from meditation —a magician always includes all four of these things: thoughts, words, emotions and actions in her/his ritual. Some people think that simply to meditate on what they want is sufficient. Yes, you can produce the same results with meditation by imagining all these aspects to be there, but it takes tremendous concentration to be able to do that effectively.

Magick rituals are basically just aids to concentration. In magick you are acting out your desires, bringing all of your senses into action, and the more "life" you can give to your desires the greater the impact they will have in the physical world.

It has been well proven in science that the human body cannot tell the difference between a thing and the thought of a thing, an action and the thought of an action. For example, a workout of a brisk two-mile jog will produce certain physiological responses: increased heart-rate, release of endorphins and hormones, oxidation of the blood and the expansion of vessels. In addition, the mind relaxes as the stresses of the day are temporarily forgotten.

Experiments have proved, time and again, that the same results are obtained by just thinking through a two-mile jog. The physical body responds just the same as if you had run those two miles. Thirty minutes of aerobic exercise will produce certain physiological responses but, again, concentrated thought of that exercise will bring about the same results.

In addition to this, frontier work in physics and biology is beginning to point to the same results for all of our physical reality. What this means is that the physical universe also responds to thoughts as if they were things. For example, if you go into your garden to weed, water and fertilize it regularly, your garden will respond with lush, healthy growth. But the garden will also respond in a like manner if, with emotion and intent, you think it green and lush!

There are many different ways to approach magick. The Egyptians approached it with high ceremony, words and formal gestures, which is the method that this book will give. As stated above, ritual is simply a method for accessing the deeper aspects of the mind and body so that the thoughts you think and the words you speak will carry the greatest amount of power that you can give them. The universe will then respond to these thoughts and set into motion the necessary responses to bring about what you have asked for.

In all magick, clarity of intention, emotion and faith are essential elements to success. It is important to remember, however, that magick does not end with the ritual. You must believe in your magick. This means that you must act as if everything you plan to have happen absolutely will happen. If you have just completed a magick ritual to bring a new love into your life, then you must behave as if it has already happened. Think about how someone who has just fallen in love feels. This involves an act of faith, and if you are not willing to do this, then you are not ready to magickally manifest your desires.

# Chapter 3

## *Magickal Groundwork*

The most important aspect of getting anything you want in life, be it through magick or through more worldly efforts, is to know specifically what it is that you really desire. This may seem simple and obvious on the surface, but the truth is that most people do not know where they would like to be on life's wheel even five years from now.

If you are young and not sure what you will be doing with your life, then at least think in general terms. For example, have you given much thought to the qualities you want to have in your life two years from now? What level of wealth? What sort of relationship? What kind of friends? Where do you want to live? How do want to feel? How do you want to look? What will your health be like?

Now is the time to develop these thoughts so that the universe can be set in motion to bring these things to you. This sort of self-examination is also important to perform before undertaking magick. Clear intent brings clear results. Fuzzy intent brings fuzzy results.

An example of an undeveloped, unclear desire would be if you decided to perform magick just because you are lonely and bored with life. You may feel that a relationship might improve the quality of your life. Self-examination, however, might reveal that your boredom with life is probably because you are boring! Under these circumstances, the relationship which you desire will elude you because other people will find you boring, too.

You cannot use love relationships to fill up empty spaces within yourself. Love is meant to be a sharing and growing experience. Love is a way to experience yourself and your world through another perspective. It is a chance to step beyond yourself, to stretch for new perspectives. Nowhere is it written that love is a way to fill your inadequacies.

Thoughts that need further examination:
*"I need someone else in order to be happy."*

A bad way to begin a relationship. That's a tall order for another person to fulfill.

What can you do to make yourself happy instead? No one is attracted to unhappy people. The most popular people are the happy ones, the ones who make you feel good when you're around them. Focus your magick on finding happiness within yourself and by yourself, so that others will be attracted to share this experience with you.

*"I am lonely. I want a relationship in order to have a friend to talk to."*

Loneliness and boredom go hand in hand. Take a detailed inventory of your life and see if you aren't just a bit boring! If you were someone else looking at your life, would you be interested in getting to know you? Figure out how you can get involved in interesting things. Make a list of different interests you have and search for ways to get involved in those things outside your home. Then, you can work magick to find a dazzling partner from one of those outside activities.

*"I am unattractive (ugly, too short, too tall, overweight, underweight, etc.) and want to be more attractive and draw a relationship into my life."*

Try to take stock of yourself from an objective position. Enlist the aid of a friend to help you see yourself clearly. Often, we feel so bad about what we perceive as a fault that we overlook many of the good qualities about ourselves. Accentuate your good points. Some people's beauty is on the outside, and some people's beauty is on the inside. Some are lucky and have it everywhere, but certainly everyone is beautiful somewhere! All of us deserve love, and there is no excuse for not having it. There are men and women, for instance, who find overlarge people unattractive, yet there are others who are very attracted to large men and women—in other words, there is someone for everyone. Your magick should focus on your personal acceptance of yourself. Strive for loving yourself even if you never change, and allow love to enter your life. This is, perhaps, especially important for people who are overweight. Do not make losing weight an issue of love. Can you love yourself even if you never change? Can you expect to be loved even if you never change? Absolutely. Go for it!

*"Relationships never last for me. I want a lasting relationship."*

Why don't your relationships last? Are you continually picking the wrong sort of person? Are you trapped in destructive behavior patterns? Are you looking for a mother or father figure? You will be doomed to continue with transitory relationships until you take a closer look at what is causing the problems—and the source is always within you. Work your magick to break these destructive patterns, work to bring another sort of person into your life, someone different from those you have had before.

*"I'm madly in love with someone, but she/he doesn't seem to know I exist."*

As I discussed before, you know it would be negative magick to try to interfere with this person's free will. Start your examination with questions such as: Why do I like this person so much? List his/her qualities that you like. Also—and this is a very tough question—ask yourself if you like to play the martyr. Do you like to fall in love with "untouchables"? Work your magick to bring a relationship with someone who has the qualities you admire. Also work to enhance these qualities in yourself.

"I'm in love with a married man/woman."

Most of these sad sagas are negative power plays. The unmarried person likes the challenge of taking someone away from someone else. Examine your life to see if there are other ways you can manifest your power. Find more satisfying ways to fulfill yourself. List the qualities you want in a mate and work your magick to bring someone unmarried.

When performing these self-examinations, be honest with yourself, but also be compassionate. Willingness to see the truth is only half of the battle; the other half is to forgive yourself. Nothing you will discover about yourself is any different, or worse, than what just about every other human has dealt with throughout history. Everyone deserves love and everyone deserves to be totally happy, and there is plenty of love and happiness to go around.

Some of you may already be involved in a good relationship, and the two of you may wish to perform magick together to strengthen your bonds. This is fine, and since you are both involved in the magick, it is not interfering with the will of another.

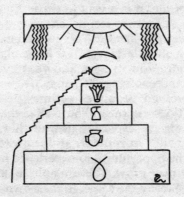

The ancient Egyptians proposed that there were four different levels of love and that these four aspects form the four corners of the pyramid—the base of life from which we grow onward to greater heights.

1. *Self-love.* Before we can love another we must first learn to love ourselves. This is why the above exercises are so important. Examine why you want a relationship. Is it just to provide you with the feeling that you are worth loving? If so, your relationships are doomed to failure or strife. Enter into love with the sure knowledge that you are worth loving. Can you list 10 reasons why you are worth loving?

2. *Love of a Significant Other.* Only after we have achieved some level of love for ourselves can we attain genuine selfless love for another human being. Only if you have learned to accept yourself with all your shortcomings and faults can you learn to accept others with theirs. Loving someone else provides you with a new perspective of yourself and of life. It is a way to expand your life, to live it more deeply, to feel richer.

3. *Love of Humanity.* This is the next, natural outgrowth of the last level. This is the place in your heart where you understand that everyone is growing and evolving. You may despise the acts that unevolved people sometimes perform, but you don't despise them. You realize that they are just growing and exploring their world (there is an implied belief in reincarnation) and that they deserve the opportunity to experience free will so that they may grow. You are able to see that all people are really the same, in their own way: each person is striving to find love and freedom from suffering. Entering this level of love expands your

participation with life even more. You become more powerful as you interact more fully with the process of life.

4. *Love of God/Goddess, All-That-Is.* This is the highest evolution of love and involves the pure love of the All-That-Is. It is a special place within us, a place of gratitude for life. When this level of love is reached, a beautiful feeling of peace, gratitude and satisfaction with life fills you. You find that you want to make commitments to the environment, to the planet, and to your fellow humans. You may suddenly develop an intense interest in global issues of peace, world hunger, the environment, or you may find an outpouring of concern for local problems such as inner city children on drugs or feeding the homeless. Perhaps you feel the urge to create great art, music or literature. The point is that the love is so intense that your gratitude and joy overflow into the world around you. You find that you want to offer back something of yourself to this energy that has given you so much. You feel utterly safe and protected. You are very powerful, for your participation with life is deeply committed. You are at peace with life.

As you have probably already guessed, we all have some mixture of all of these levels of loving working within us at all times. But there are percentages that you will sense. You ought to be able to sense where you spend most of your time on this ladder. If you find that you are at level one, then relax and don't try to force yourself to another level until you are ready.

The ladder can provide guidance to approaching problems in love. For example, if you are currently involved in a relationship and find that you are insecure and jealous, look to your foundation (level one). Are you insecure about yourself? Can you trust yourself? Do you like yourself? Answering these questions may provide some amazing solutions for the relationship problem you are having on level two.

Perhaps that most powerful summation of magickal practice can be applied here. It is a very important law and states:

*The steps to getting there are the qualities of being there.*

Likewise, the reverse is true:

*The qualities of being there are the steps to getting there.*

This isn't really as much of a brain twister as it sounds. It is basically saying that if you know what you want and wonder how to get it, examine what it would be like to be there and put those qualities in your life now.

Before you continue on to the next chapter, be sure you have examined your motives and pinpointed exactly what it is that you wish to accomplish with your Love Charm. Write out several simple sentences stating what your objective is. Write a second sentence stating how you will magickally approach this desire. Be specific and brief. For example:

"I want to bring a new boyfriend into my life. He will be close to my age, free from other relationships and share my interests in photography, hiking and going to the movies."

"I will work to overcome my shyness by going out and meeting new people. I will infuse myself with confidence that I am an interesting person—one who is worth sharing with."

Or, perhaps:

"I want a special, loving relationship with an attractive woman who thinks I am good looking. I will work to see myself as attractive to women. I will work to give myself confidence to approach women."

# Chapter 4

## *Preparations For Making Your Love Charm*

**Knot Magick**

The Priests and Priestesses of Isis have been using magickal knots for thousands of years. Basically, when you tie a knot you seal in a desire or wish. There are many different types of knot magick. In some types you seal the power into the knot to store as energy that you can release later by untying the knot. Sailors used to buy "wind knots" from the Priests to take to sea and use when the winds died.

*Protection*       *Power*      *Health, Strength, Virility*

The Love Charm that you are going to be making is in the form of a necklace (and it can be worn by both female and male). It is different from a regular necklace in that, as with Egyptian magick, it incorporates knots that have been tied magickally.

Each knot is separated by a bead. The knot seals in the desire; the bead amplifies or charges the desire; so both knots and beads are important, working together. The love charm becomes a storer of energy. When the necklace is finished, and the two ends are connected together, it will be as if you have plugged the necklace into an energy source. The circuit is complete and fully charged. It creates its own energy field of attraction and amplifies your aura when you wear it. The more you wear the Charm, the more powerful it becomes.

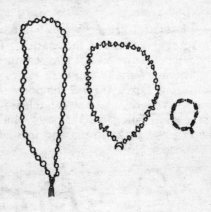

## Queen Cleopatra's Love Charm

Cleopatra was not only a great queen but also famous for her romances. It is interesting to note that historians claim she was not a beautiful woman. Busts and drawings of Cleopatra are not particularly flattering, which has led to much speculation as to how she could become so famous for her lovers.

As with all the queens of Egypt, Cleopatra was a Priestess of Isis and well schooled in Egyptian magick. The following illustration is taken from a very old Love Charm currently in the possession of one of the secret societies of Isis. This Love Charm is said to have belonged to Cleopatra, indeed it is reputed to have been made by her own hand. Could it be that Cleopatra's great secret in attracting men was that she was a powerful magician? This doesn't mean that she deceived them, it just means she believed in herself and was powerful enough to take action on this belief.

*Cleopatra's Love Charm, gold beads with ivory lotus*

The story still being told relates that, near the end of her life and while in a great depression, Cleopatra tossed her Love Charm into the Nile. The Charm had brought her great love but could not control the powerful political tides of the Roman Empire.

A servant named Nanua, also a Priest of Isis, was with his queen when she threw her charm into the river. But Nanua also saw that the charm landed in the papyrus reeds near the shore, and later crept back to claim the charm—hoping it would bring him love.

It is not known whether or not the Charm brought Nanua love, but at the time of his death he passed it on to the temple to keep as a treasured remembrance of a great Queen. (Many of the secret societies of Isis have treasuries containing priceless items such as this.)

## The Spell

The technique used to lock your desire within the knot is to physically tie a knot (which will be explained in detail in Part II of this book) while saying your spell. The spell should express your goal in simple terms and, if possible, should rhyme.

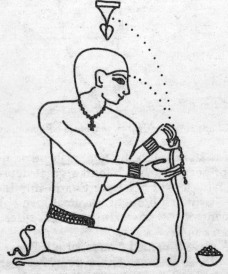

Rhyming is a very old technique for accessing deeper portions of your mind. Rhyming allows you to more easily enter a trance state which can be very helpful to attaining the proper working state to create your magick.

Some rules to remember for creating a spell formula:

1. Keep it simple and your goal precise.
2. Make it rhyme.
3. Keep your approach positive.
4. Use present or present perfect tense as much as possible. For example: "I am ..." or "I am becoming..."
5. Be poetic and emotional if you wish—it can only help.

Examples:

This may be the spell of a tall young man who feels he is unattractive:

> *"True love comes and I am free*
> *Of all life's trivialities;*
> *I see myself as tall and fair*
> *With joyous heart to grow and share.*
> *This charm is bound, so mote it be."*

This may be the spell of a woman who hasn't had any luck with keeping a serious relationship in her life:

> *"Warm, loving energy surrounds me,*
> *astounds me,*
> *Old patterns drift away like leaves in the*
> *wind,*
> *And I am found wanting, confronting my*
> *new life,*
> *Opening new windows and drawing love*
> *in!"*

Before you go further, please prepare your own individualized spell for your Love Charm.

## Timing

To the Egyptians, timing was one of the most important aspects of magick. The Egyptian year had 12 months which were each 30 days long. The year was divided into three seasons: spring, summer and winter, and was 360 days long. The five extra days left at the end of the year were known as "the five days over the year" and were a time of celebration and relaxation, sort of like an Egyptian New Year.

The Egyptians felt quite strongly about astrology and propitious timing. It is uncertain how much of today's complex astrology was used by the ancient Egyptians, but we do know that any planned event, be it magickal or mundane, was carefully coordinated with the seasons of the Earth in relation to the Sun, Moon and planets.

Life in Egypt has always been overshadowed by the natural seasons of the great Nile River. The Egyptians felt that all of nature responded to, and worked with, the seasons of the year. They noticed that the animals followed the seasons very closely. The seasons told the animals when it was time to mate, to build a nest, and to bear young, just as it tells humans when to mate, plant the grain, harvest and rest. So it naturally followed that spring was the most auspicious time to work love magick.

Are you reading this book in the middle of summer and anxious to make your Love Charm? Are you afraid you might have to wait until next spring to do so? Although spring is a powerful season to work love magick, there are other times during the year that are also meaningful to you.

New Year's, for instance, can be a refreshing time to end old relationships and begin new ones or to turn over a new leaf and bring fresh things into your life. Steamy midsummer nights can be a romantic inspiration. Also, remember, if you are wanting to weed yourself of destructive love pat-

terns, then perhaps winter would be the best time
to begin your love charm. In this way, by the time
spring arrives you have had ample time to work
out your inner changes so that a new relationship
can step into your life.

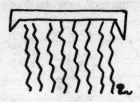

*Winter* (Akhet): The season of rest. This is traditionally a good time to rest and do inner work.
This is the best time to change inner attitudes. It is
good for psychic work—for planning ahead.

*Spring* (Piruit): The season of "coming forth."
This is the season of sowing new seeds. It is the
season of new beginnings, new relationships.

*Summer* (Shemut): This is the time of fulfillment. Life is at its fullest—ripe with promise. It is the season of passion!

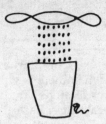

*Autumn*: The season of harvest. When all that you have sown comes to fruition. This is an excellent time to weed out those old negative emotional patterns that have been interfering with your relationships. Clean up your garden and prepare it for the winter snows.

In addition to the influence of the seasons, it is very important to observe solar and lunar energies.

Solar associations:

*Sunrise*: Beginnings, the start of new love.

*Noon*: Fruition of plans. (Not a good time to do magick.)

*Sunset*: Inward seeking. A good time to work love magick for spiritual goals.

*Midnight*: The best time to work most magick as the Egyptians considered night to be a return to the womb of creation. You are giving birth to your desire and will bring it into the light.

Lunar associations:

*New Moon*: This is the darkest night of the month, the night when there is virtually no Moon at all—just a sliver of silver. Traditionally, it is a time of inward searching. Basically, only people who wish to induce conception should perform their magick now.

*Waxing Moon*: This is any time that the Moon is growing from the New Moon toward the Full Moon. Any magick done during this waxing Moon period would be geared toward bringing something to you. Although this is a fine time to work magick, it is not as powerful as right at the Full Moon.

*Full Moon*: This is the best time to perform most types of love magick. Your psychic energies are at their peak and magick will be easier for you. If you have any doubt when to perform your magick, this is always the safest bet.

*Waning Moon*: This should only be used if you are needing to focus on removing something from your life. If you are in a very unpleasant relationship and wish to leave it and start over, try starting your beads during the waning Moon and finishing them during the waxing Moon. Since the point of this book is to bring love into your life, it would not be appropriate to exclusively use just the waning Moon, for that would only be drawing things away from you.

Other than the influence of the seasons, Sun

and Moon, you can use basic astrological information about the planets to help you pick a good day to create your magickal love charm. For example, maybe you would like to give yourself a birthday present by working the charm on your birthday!

## Numerology

The Egyptians were very great believers in the power of numbers. In numerology, everything is given a numerical value but, most commonly, it is the letters of the alphabet which are of primary importance. It is not known what number the Egyptians assigned to each hieroglyphic figure, and even if we did know, it would be impossible to translate a numeric equivalent into our own alphabet so it is recommended that you follow the standard, modern number assignation:

| 1 | 2 | 3 | 4 | 5 | 6 | 7 | 8 | 9 |
|---|---|---|---|---|---|---|---|---|
| A | B | C | D | E | F | G | H | I |
| J | K | L | M | N | O | P | Q | R |
| S | T | U | V | W | X | Y | Z |   |

To use this chart, simply assign each letter of the alphabet to the number at the top of the vertical row. For example, the name Susan would be:

$$S + U + S + A + N =$$
$$1 + 3 + 1 + 1 + 5 = 11$$

$$11 = 1 + 1 = 2$$

As you can see, all compound numbers are

reduced to a single digit by adding the numbers together. For example 38 become $3 + 8 = 11$, which in turn becomes $1 + 1 = 2$. So the number 38 is a "number 2." Likewise, the number 143 is $1 + 4 + 3$ which equals 8, so the number 143 is a "number 8."

A common number which is important in numerology is your birth or life cycle number. To obtain this number, simply add all the numbers in your birth date.

Example:

Birthday: March 19, 1955. March is the third month so the calculation would look like this:

March 19, 1955 = $3 + 1 + 9 + 1 + 9 + 5 + 5 = 33 = 3 + 3 = 6$

The life cycle number of a person born on March 19, 1955 is 6.

Another calculation important to numerologists is your name number. This is obtained by adding all the letters in your name to come up with a single digit. It is considered best to use whatever name you most commonly are known by, even if it is a nickname. It is also considered important that your name number vibrate in harmony with your life cycle number. The significance of the nine basic numbers are as follows:

1. Purpose, action, ambition, aggression, leadership.
2. Balance, passivity, receptivity, harmony.
3. Versatility, gaiety, brilliance.
4. Steadiness, endurance, foundations, dullness.
5. Adventure, instability, expansion, sexuality.
6. Dependability, harmony, beauty, love,

domesticity.

7. Mystery, knowledge, solitariness, dreaming.

8. Material success, worldly achievement, power.

9. Great achievement, inspiration, spirituality (spirit balanced in the material world).

If you are interested in numerology, you can pick a day that adds up to a 6 (the number of Venus) by adding together the month, day and year. For example May 26, 1991 can be added as follows: 5 (May is the 5th month) + 2 + 6 + 1 + 9 + 9 + 1 = 33 which is 3 + 3 = 6. So May 26, 1991 would be a good day for working your love magick.

Before progressing beyond this chapter, decide when would be a good time for you to work your Love Charm.

8- 27- 1933

- 33 ≤ 6

363÷12= 3

35553375 = 36 = 9

*Part II*

# Chapter 5

## *The Tools*

Before collecting your beads, you must prepare other items that will be important in the construction of your magickal charm—the ritual tools, or the magician's tools.

It is traditional that a magickal tool be made by the hand of the magician who will use it. However, it is generally accepted that any ordinary object may be converted by simply putting a little of your own energy into it. This is usually done by cleansing, changing or decorating the object in some way to make it personal to the magician. In other words, you can add some of your own creative energy to an ordinary object and imbue it with power by giving it purpose.

Magicians believe that all things are alive. What most people in our society would label as "inanimate" the magician sees as alive. Rocks and plants, as well as animals and people, are all alive with thoughts and feelings. Cars, clothes and even televisions also carry a certain life force inside them.

There are different levels of "aliveness," and it is generally thought that the more natural an object is (one that occurs naturally in nature), the more life energy it has. So it would follow that a magician would choose to make her/his wand from a tree branch rather than a plastic rod because it would have more life energy within it and would be more powerful to work with magickally.

Because all things are alive, they can be directed or given a purpose. A magician creates a tool by
putting his/her directive thoughts into the object
so that it becomes imbued with these thoughts.

You will need very few, special tools to make
your charm. Most of these items you will be using
will be magickally altered by cleaning them with
salt and anointing them with oil. Making your own
magickal salts and oil will be the most important
preparation you can do, for it is these two items
that will help you transform common, everyday
items into powerful, magickal tools. By preparing
the salt and oil yourself, you can imbue them with
your own desires and use ingredients that will add
influential energies to what work you wish to do.

**Love Oil**

Magickal oils have been used for thousands of years, and are one of the basic cornerstones of magick, especially love magick. Oils are easy to make but must be prepared in advance as they must "brew" for a while. This is one of the most important items you will use for your Love Charm, so be sure to follow the instructions carefully and do not attempt to "cut corners" to save time.

"Nile Nights Oil" (Traditional)
*This is a standard, all-purpose, general love oil.*

1 clean jar or bottle
Cheesecloth or fine mesh strainer
4 ounces of a light salad or cooking oil*
3 whole vanilla pods (found in grocery or health food stores)
1 vitamin E capsule (optional)
1 small crystal (optional)

*For best results, it is recommended that you use an unrefined, cold-pressed oil such as what is found in health food stores. Magickally speaking, the less something has been processed, the more powerful it will be for you—and it is also healthier to use on your skin.

Pour the oil into a clean pan and add the vanilla pods. Gently heat the oil and spice for about 20 minutes then allow to cool for an hour. Pour into the jar or bottle and add the capsule of Vitamin E, to help the oil remain fresh (not needed if you have used a refined oil). Add the E by poking through the skin of the capsule with a pin and squeezing the vitamin into the oil. Seal and shake well. Keep the jar at the back of the stove or some other warm place in the house for about 3 days, shaking several times each day. At the end of the 3 days you may then strain the oil through cheesecloth, or a fine strainer, pour back into the jar and store in a cool place. (If the scent is not strong enough for you, leave the pods in the jar for a longer period of time. Also, the scent will continue to strengthen even after the pods are removed.)

It's also nice to add a small crystal that you have charged with your love desires to the bottle of oil. To do this simply cleanse the crystal with salt and water, bless it by acknowledging its connection to the Divine Source, and then charge it by telling it what you want it to do for you. All stones have good memories. Crystals not only remember but also energize, so if you tell the crystal what you want it to do, it will remember what you have said and add its energy to this end.

"Passion's Quest Oil"
(Also known as "Kitchen Love Oil")
*This recipe specializes in arousing erotic passion to spice up your life. Men often like to use this oil as it doesn't smell too feminine, just spicy.*

1 clean jar or bottle
Cheesecloth
1 cup of suitable oil
1 1/2 tsp. powdered cinnamon
1 tsp. powdered cardamom
3 whole cloves
3 drops of pure vanilla extract
2 tsp. powdered myrrh (optional)
1 capsule of vitamin E oil
1 small crystal (optional)

Add the herbs, oil and vitamin E into the clean jar or bottle. Seal tightly and allow it to sit in sunlight for 14 days. Shake the jar at least once each day. After 14 days remove the jar from the sunlight and store in complete darkness for 14 days. Do not shake during this second 14 days, just leave it alone. At the end of the time, strain ingredients through a cheesecloth and back into your jar. You may add your crystal at this time, if you wish. Store in a cool place.

It is best to begin this recipe at the Full Moon and finish on the following Full Moon. The oil will gain in potency as the Moon completes a full cycle.

Another method for making an aromatic oil is by adding essential oils to your basic salad oil. This method is quicker, you don't have to steep the oil, but it is more expensive as essential oils can be costly. There are many oils on the market, if you choose this method, make sure that the oil you use is a pure essential oil.

### "Love Oil"

Simply mix the essential oil of your choice with your salad oil. Add the essential oil a drop at a time as it is very, very strong. You will probably need only a few drops for 6 ounces of oil. The essential oils are so strong that most of them smell bad when sniffed straight from the bottle and undiluted. Don't be put off by this. Once the essential oil is diluted, it again becomes recognizable and pleasant.

When mixing the oils, be sure not to shake or stir; simply swirl the contents around.

The following essential oils may be used individually or as a blend to create a super fine love oil. All of these scents are traditional in love magick.

Apple (For new or young love)
Gardenia (For women, an aphrodisiac)
Geranium (A less expensive substitute for rose, general love energy)
Hibiscus (An aphrodisiac)
Jasmine (Very expensive, but works well for men or women)
Lavender (Good for men as it's not too sweet, brings new love)
Lotus (For men or women, very sacred to the

Egyptians)

Mimosa (For women only! Highly evocative)

Neroli (Orange Blossom, also very expensive but
wonderful for either men or women, removes
love blockages)

Rose (Very expensive, mostly for women, high
love energy)

Vanilla (Effective for men or women, strong aphrodisiac)

Ylang-Ylang (Very sweet, brings goodness, light
and love)

## Sacred Salt Mixture

The next important item to create is the salt, as
this will be used in many other preparations.

Salt was a very magickal purifier to the
Egyptians. They used it as a drying and purifying
agent for embalming. They used it to wash down
their temples, bless holy water, charge magickal
charms and shoo away evil spirits. Salt was probably one of the very first cleansing agents ever used.

As in all things magickal, it is not the ordinary
salt that is used but rather a specially cooked-up
recipe. The following recipes are currently used by
Egyptian Priestesses. Choose any one, or more.

## "Modern Priest/ess Salt"
*This is quick and easy. Use your favorite perfume or cologne that makes you feel especially sexy.*

6 rounded teaspoons of table salt
1/4 to 1/2 teaspoon of your favorite perfume or cologne
1 to 2 drops of red food coloring (to attain pink color)
1 crystal, preferably rose quartz (leave whole!)

During the waxing Moon (when the Moon is getting bigger) when the Sun touches the horizon (either dawn or dusk), combine the above ingredients in a glass bowl and mix well with a plastic or wooden spoon. Let no metal touch the ingredients. Store in a glass, earthenware or wooden jar. Avoid metal or plastic. Add your crystal to the mixture to charge it with your purpose. Any type of crystal will do, but rose quartz is traditional.

## "Ancient Echoes Salt"
*This is a traditional recipe said to have been discovered in the Temple of Isis in Pompeii.*

6 rounded teaspoons of sea salt (rock or table variety)
3/4 teaspoon of ground cloves
1 teaspoon of cinnamon powder
1/4 teaspoon of myrrh powder (optional)
3 allspice balls
1 crystal or sacred stone (your choice), leave whole

At the Full Moon after the Sun has set, light a white candle and a stick of incense to Isis. Mix the above ingredients in a glass bowl using a plastic or wooden spoon. Let no metal touch the contents. Charge the crystal or stone with your love request and mix with the rest of the salt. Hold your salt mixture up to the heavens and, in your own words, ask Isis to bless these salts to purify your work.

"Garden of Hearts Salt"
*This recipe comes from a modern Isian temple in Great Britain. It is reputedly used for romantic quests.*

6 rounded teaspoons of table or rock salt
1 to 2 drops of red food coloring (to attain pink color)
1 package of your favorite simmering potpourri mixture (which can be found in your local drugstore)

Light a pink candle at midnight. Spend a moment or two thinking about the love that you desire. Visualize walking through a secret garden in the moonlight. Ask the flower spirits to infuse your Love Salts with their special magickal essences to bring love, light and joy into your life. Mix the ingredients together and store in an air-tight jar.

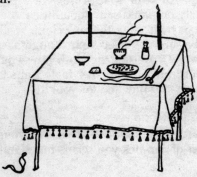

**Magical Table/Altar Cloth**

You will need to think about what you will be using as your table. If you will be calling upon Isis during your charm-making, then you can look upon this as an altar. Whether you see it as an altar or as a table does not matter, but it should be regarded as something special and holy. It represents your foundation; it is the base from which you build your magick. The table is your miniature universe from which you will work your desires into a magickal object.

To actually construct a special, magickal altar is a very large project, which is why most Magicians simply use a special tablecloth that they put over an ordinary table or chest-of-drawers to convert into their altar. The tablecloth may be of pink or red to signify love or passion, or it may be white, which contains all the colors of the rainbow. Or, if your prefer, you may use an attractive Egyptian-looking print. If you do not have a tablecloth in the house, you can usually find one in your neighborhood thrift store for a modest amount of money.

To specially cleanse and charge your tablecloth you should wash it (either by hand or by machine) and, along with your soap, throw in a pinch of your specially prepared salt. Put a little more energy into things by ironing the tablecloth. While you iron it, make sure you keep your thoughts on how special this cloth is—tell the cloth how you have picked it out from all the other tablecloths to perform a very special function for you!

**Candles**

You will need at least two candles on your altar. The number of candles you use is not significant, but at least two are suggested so that you can have enough light to see what you are doing when you make your charm. Some people use a semicircle of rainbow candles on the altar to cover all aspects of love and to give lots of illumination to their work. You may choose tall or short, tapers or votive; it matters not, so long as they are properly "dressed."

To dress a candle you must anoint it with your specially made oil. Concentrate on your desire while you are anointing it. Use your forefinger (Goddess finger) to rub the oil well into the candle, including the top and the bottom. Be sure to have clean candleholders for them.

The following are some colors you may wish to use and their symbolism.

White: All-encompassing light and love. Spiritual love.
Pink: Emotional love. Joy
Red: Passion. Energetic love, physical love.
Blue: Peace, serenity. Love of children.
Purple: Gratitude. Love of Higher Self.
Green: Love for animals.
Gold/Yellow: Wisdom, guiding love.

**Incense**

Stick incense is fine, or even incense cones. There may be some of you, however, who wish to make your own powdered incense. This will require that you purchase special charcoal briquettes that are specially manufactured for use with incense. These can be purchased either in metaphysical bookstores, botanicals or at religious supply stores. You will need a strong ceramic bowl filled with sand to diffuse the heat of the charcoal. Never use the charcoal without sand, and do not try to use barbecue charcoal as it is toxic when lit indoors. You will also need small pliers, tongs or tweezers to hold the briquette while lighting it so that you don't burn yourself.

If you are purchasing incense sticks or cones, any one of the following scents is usually easy to obtain and has long been associated with love:

Rose
Sandalwood
Jasmine
Vanilla
Cinnamon

If you do not have an incense holder, a small bowl with sand or earth will hold the sticks or cones.

For those who wish to make their own powdered incense to use with the charcoal, here are some traditional recipes:

"Temple Incense"
(*From a temple of Isis*)

Cedar
Myrrh

Calamus
Juniper
Frankincense
Cinnamon
Cassia

No proportions were given for this mixture, only the admonition to "go easy on the frankincense." Use your own nose as guidance.

"Kyphi Incense"

This is a very traditional incense that has been used for thousands of years in Egypt. It is not known exactly what all of the original ingredients were, and so many of the modern recipes vary. Generally, however, the following items are found. Again, it is up to you to mix the proportions according to your own taste.

Benzoin
Frankincense
Cinnamon
Calamus
Cassia
Galangal
Juniper Berries
Mastic
Cedar
Cypress
Cardamom
Myrrh
Lotus Oil
Orris
Wine
Honey

When mixing your own incenses, you may need a mortar and pestle to grind some of the gums and resins into smaller pieces. Use your fingers to mix the ingredients together so that you infuse it with your energy. Store in an airtight jar in a cool, dark place. (Light and heat leach energy from herbs.)

**Water, Salt and Oil Dishes**
Have three small dishes prepared in which you will put your special salt, your water and your oil. Be sure these dishes are clean and ready for the time when you construct your charm.

**Robe**

Although some magicians go to a lot of extra effort to make a special robe to do magick in, it is not necessary. It is best to wear clean, loose clothing that is not restrictive. This means that you do not want to restrict the flow of blood or energy. Traditionally, this has meant a simple garment with little or no underclothing. You may use as much imagination as you like. If you can find clothing suggestive of Egyptian clothes, so much the better. Sometimes a plain white bed sheet can look pretty good when belted.

The important point is to prepare the garment with a special wash, using your magickal salts, and to set it aside only for magickal use, or at least until you have completed your Love Charm.

# Chapter 6

## *Beads*

Before you gather together your beading tools, it is a good idea to have chosen what sort of bead you wish to use and how you will be wearing your charm. If you want to wear your charm as an anklet, you will need to use smaller beads than you might use for a necklace or bracelet. Large beads around the ankle would not only look strange, but would also be uncomfortable.

**For Men**

The Isian clergy was fairly evenly divided between men and women, and men were known to make use of this Love Charm as frequently as women. Jewelry was more commonly worn by men in ancient times, but don't let that deter you from wearing one now. If you wear a suit and tie, it will never even show. Attractive, masculine-looking charms can be made by carefully choosing colors and materials that are not considered "effeminate." Wood, hematite, leopard jasper, bloodstone, amber and garnet are some stones you might consider trying. Men most commonly make their Love Charm as a bracelet or necklace.

The size of the bead and the size of the hole in the bead will dictate the needle and string size. You might even want to consider what color string you wish to use.

There are several things to consider in choosing a bead: color, material (what the bead is made of), affordability and availability. Below are listed some tables that will give you guidance on the various influences to be found in the different colors and materials.

## Colors

Red:     Strength, Health, Vigor, Sexual Love, Energy

Orange:     Attraction, Stimulation, Encouragement, Joy

Yellow:     Persuasion, Cleansing, Renewal, Comfort, Warmth

Green:     Fertility, Prosperity, Growth, Balance

Blue:     Devotion, Sincerity, Tranquility, Truth

Indigo:     Freedom, Compassionate Detachment, Unconditional Love

Violet:     Spiritual Love, Spiritual Fire, Soothing

Pink:     Emotional Love, Relaxation, Purifier

Purple:     Gratitude, Spiritual Enrichment

Brown:     Love of Nature, Love of Animals, Security

Grey:     Friendship

Black:     Seeking Light or Understanding, Resolutions

Clear:     Energy Boosters, Amplifiers, Neutral

White:     Purity, Creativity, Psychic Powers, Moon Energy

## Materials

Wood:     Strength, Sustenance, Support, Endurance

Shell:     Emotions, Rebirthing, Love, Cleansing

Glass:     Insulation, Clarity, Communication

Stone:     Wisdom, Growth, Grounding

Metal:     Communication, Amplification, Protection

Plastic: Intellect, Travel, Fluidity, Change

## Minerals

You can put together your own combinations of color and material to find the bead that is just right for you, but below are listed some examples of beads that have been popular as Love Charms for thousands of years, along with their traditional meanings:

*Coral*: Sacred to Isis, this is a superb Love Charm bead that has been used since prehistoric times. Using the chart above, choose the color that most fits your needs (white, orange, red or pink).

*Rose Quartz*: This stone is an excellent Love bead as it combines wisdom with emotional love. It is grounding and relaxing.

*Amber*: This is another very ancient love stone (which really falls under the category of wood since it is actually the resin of wood rather than a stone). It is soothing to the physical body, yet it aids in stirring up physical love. It is both arousing, balancing and soothing all at the same time. It spirals your energy upward and is sacred to the Great Serpent who, according to the ancient Egyptians, taught the art of physical love to humans.

*Amethyst*: This has long been used as the stone of spiritual love. To be a stone of spiritual love, however, it must contain all the other aspects of love within it from self-love to physical love to love of another, all the way up to love of God/Goddess/All-That-Is and all humanity. This is not the stone to be used for just earthly love, but if you aspire to spiritual growth as well as earthly love, then none can surpass it.

*Sandalwood*: This is an especially good bead for men as it stimulates male sexuality, although women could wear it to stimulate men. It is also known as a very powerful healer and dispeller of negativity. Although perhaps not terribly attractive as a necklace, it can be a very potent source of Love magick!

*Garnet*: This stone is a stimulator so it has been used for sexual stimulation as well as a physical healer for the heart. It purifies the blood and is believed to keep lovers true to one another.

*Gold*: Gold has been highly prized since the beginning of civilization. It is an unsurpassed energy conductor and, when directed, can bring in Love energies that will send your head reeling! Be careful for it must be given direction (purpose) to do it's task properly. Hollow (very light weight) gold beads are not as expensive as you might think. If you cannot afford to have all gold beads on your charm, you might consider using them as occasional spacers between your other beads.

## Astrological Associations

| Zodiac | Color | Metal | Stone |
|---|---|---|---|
| Aries | Red | Iron | Bloodstone, Red Jasper, Ruby |
| Taurus | Yellow | Copper | Topaz, Emerald, Coral |
| Gemini | Violet | Mercury | Crystal, Carbuncle |
| Cancer | Green | Silver | Moonstone |
| Leo | Orange | Gold | Ruby, Sardonyx, Amber |
| Virgo | Violet | Mercury | Pink Jasper, Turquoise |
| Libra | Yellow | Copper | Opal, Diamond |
| Scorpio | Red | Iron | Agate, Garnet, Topaz |
| Sagittarius | Purple | Tin | Amethyst |
| Capricorn | Blue | Lead | Black & White Onyx, Jet |
| Aquarius | Indigo | Lead | Blue Sapphire |
| Pisces | Indigo | Tin | Jade |

## Numerology

Earlier we spoke of 6 as being the number of Venus. Tradition says that the number of beads you have on your Love Charm should always be reducible to the number 6 or a number divisible into 6. What does this mean? In numerology basically you only work with the single digits. After 9 the numbers begin to repeat themselves in different combinations—10 is just a combination of a 1 and a 0. You add the two numbers together to produce the single number. In this case 10 becomes 1 + 0 = 1; 94 becomes 9 + 4 = 13, which becomes 1 + 3 = 4. You can always reduce any number to a single digit by this method.

To have a number that reduces to 6 means that you can have 24, 33, 42, etc., beads on your necklace.

As you can see, the number 6 can be rather restrictive, which is why you may also use a number that is divisible into 6—which would be 2 or 3. 2 would be the next best choice as it, too, is a number of love. 3 is acceptable, but it deals more with the love of joy and friendship rather than a one-on-one relationship. This opens up your choices of the number of beads a bit more, for in addition to the above numbers you may also use numbers like: 20, 29, 38, etc., which all reduce to the number 2, or numbers such as 21, 30, 39, etc which reduce to the number 3.

Where can you find your beads? You can cannibalize old necklaces and cut them up (you *will* have to cut them up—you can't just use them as they are since the magick is in the knotwork that you will be doing). You can also purchase loose beads at a bead store or through a bead catalogue.

Don't let your intellect do all the selecting. The charts above are just to provide a little guidance. Let your intuition be your selector. Go with what feels right to you.

## Bead Shape and Size

Be careful about the shape of your beads. Sometimes the least expensive beads are made of mineral chips that have been tumbled. Are these going to be comfortable for you to use? Usually round beads are easier in the long run, for you will be fingering the beads as you say your magickal chant. Also, the round beads are more comfortable when worn for long periods of time next to the skin. If you feel comfortable with the chips, however, then that is fine. Also, it is important that your beads be approximately all the same size as you do not want one to stand out over the others.

Review:

Think about the color of the bead you will use. Think about the material (the energy), the shape, and the size. Work out the best number of beads to use.

# Chapter 7

## *Beading Supplies*

*Tools Needed*:
Scissors
Tweezers (sharp-pointed ones are especially helpful)

*Supplies Needed*:
Slim beading needle
Thread
Beeswax
Bead Dish
Beads
End fob
Clear Nail Polish or Glue

*Scissors and Tweezers*:
The tools, scissors and tweezers, are self-explanatory. It is possible to do the knots between the beads without using tweezers if you do not have them. The tweezers just make it easier.

*Beading Needles*:
Bead stores and some sewing or hobby stores sell special beading needles. These are by far the easiest to work with, but really any needle which is slim enough to get through the beads you have chosen for your Charm will do.

*Thread*:

Bead stores also sell special beading thread in different thicknesses. This thread usually comes in many different colors and materials. Nylon and silk are the most common. If you buy the spool, your color choice is usually white or black. Most bead stores sell little silk or nylon packets containing a threaded beading needle and about 72 inches of thread. These are usually available in a wide variety of colors. In a pinch, however, heavy cotton rug thread that you can purchase at the sewing store will work just fine, although you will have to double the thread.

*Beeswax*:

If you think you will ever be doing any other beadwork, it is very important to purchase beeswax. It is used to wax the thread, which is imperative for keeping your work tangle-free. However, if this is just a one-time Charm for you, try using waxed dental floss for your thread. This is already waxed and will prevent you from having to buy the beeswax. Whether you use beeswax or waxed dental floss is not important, but do not attempt to do any beadwork without any wax, or you will just end up with a knotted mess. The wax will keep your thread from knotting.

*Bead Dish*:

You will need a shallow dish in which to put the beads. Have the beads counted out ahead of time so that you have the exact number ready.

*End Fob*:

Your strand of Love Charm beads will need to have some sort of beginning/end point on them.

A small gold or silver symbol such as a heart, of the type found on a charm bracelet, is common. Some people use a larger bead to indicate the end, and still others have made colorful tassels to attach to the end.

You can make a colorful tassel by using regular sewing thread. Combine colors to create a pleasing effect. Choose one or more colors that you would like to use in your tassel, then use a small piece of cardboard to wrap the threads around.

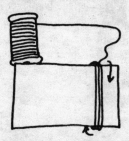

When you have attained the thickness you desire, carefully slip the thread off the cardboard and wrap another piece of thread several times around the tassel threads. Tie a knot and leave two strands several inches long that you can attach to your Love Charm.

Now bunch the threads together and wind more thread around to form the head of the tassel. Tie off. (See A.)

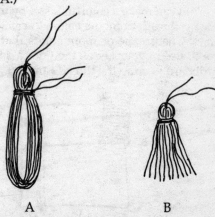

A                                        B

Finish your tassel by cutting the end threads to form the fringe. Trim to desired length. (See B.)

## Nail Polish / Glue:

The clear nail polish or glue is used to seal your beginning and ending knot so that it will hold and will not become unraveled.

Now that you have everything ready, the actual construction of the charm will be described in detail. These are the steps that you will be taking as part of your Magickal Ritual—to actually construct your Egyptian Love Charm (Part III, Chapter 9). It is recommended that you do at least a few practice knots, with beads, before you begin the Charm Ritual itself. The knotting between each bead is a difficult and time-consuming job, and it will serve you well to practice first. (Details below.)

**How To Assemble**
(This will be done as part of the actual ritual, of course. But read this through so that you know what you will be doing. Practice, if you wish, with similar beads, thread, etc.)

**1.** Wax your thread, if you are not using dental floss.
**2.** Measure how long you want your charm necklace. You will need your thread to be seven times that length, plus 6 more inches. (Knotting takes up a tremendous amount of thread space.)
**3.** Leaving about 6 inches hanging free, tie the ends together several times and add a drop of clear nail polish or glue. Do not cut the end of the string off; you will need it later.

**4.** Add your first bead and make your first knot: a loose overhand knot with the thread.

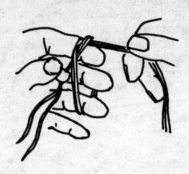

**5.** Place your tweezers through the knot and, at the same time, grasp the thread next to the beads. Slowly tighten the knot around the tweezer points when the knot is near the bead. Remove the tweezers.

**6.** Place the tweezers to the side of the knot farthest from the bead, press gently inwards and tighten the knot firmly to secure the knot against the bead. Remember, when you come to do this in the ritual itself, you will be directing your spell into each knot as you tie it.

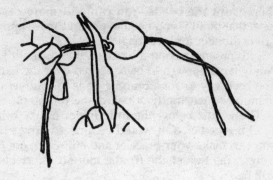

Note: Some people find it easier to use their fingers rather than the tweezers, and some find it easier to use the tweezers. This is why it is important to practice this technique before you actually begin your love charm.

**7.** Continue to add the beads individually and repeat steps 4 through 6 until all the beads have been strung.

**8.** After you have placed the knot behind the last bead, then place the fob, tassel or end bead on your charm. Finish by tying the two ends together and sealing the knot with the nail polish or glue.

Keep in mind that if your beads are to be in the form of a necklace it will need to be long enough to slip over the head. It is hard to estimate in advance exactly how many beads this will take. If you are working with numerology, be aware that you will have to work some of the numbers out during the ritual as you come to the completion of the charm. Make the charm long enough to fit over your head, then count the beads. You can add more beads from that point if you need to obtain a more appropriate number for love magick.

If you are making a bracelet, then make it just barely large enough to be squeezed over the hand. The best way to get a bracelet on is to contract the palm by squeezing (just below the thumb on one side, and just below the little finger on the other side) it together. You would be amazed how small you can make your bracelet and still get it on. (Of course, the tighter the fit, the more comfortable it will be.)

If you wish to make an anklet, you will need to use a clasp to get it on and off. It is fairly easy to obtain one from a bead store or a jeweler, or you can recycle one from an old bracelet or necklace. Simply tie it on and use a drop of glue or nail polish to seal the knot. Your end fob can be placed on either side of the clasp.

# Chapter 8

## *Final Preparations*

As the day and time you have chosen to create your Love Charm approaches, you will need to make these last-minute preparations before beginning your ritual.

Read the ritual in the next chapter to make sure that you are fully prepared before beginning. Have your altar set up and your magickal robe laid out. Likewise, all your beads and beading tools should be in place on your altar. You might want to consider taking your phone off the hook if you are going to perform this ritual at a time of day when it could disturb you.

### Preparation of the Inner Body

One important consideration in your preparations is food. The Egyptian custom is strict about this: a partial fast should be observed for 12 hours prior to the ritual. The restrictions read as follows:

No animal flesh

No animal product (milk, eggs, butter, etc.)

No drugs (coffee, tea, alcohol, medications)

Recommended foods:

Fruits
Vegetables
Biscuits
Water

The Egyptians were not vegetarians, but they felt that emotions could be heightened by the prescribed diet. If, for medical reasons, you are not comfortable with the above diet, then simply try to eat as lightly as possible during the 12 hours preceding your ritual.

## Altar Set-Up

The altar is where you will perform the ritual and make the charm. It is your table and your offering. Pay special attention to how you put it together so that it reflects your deepest desires.

By now, you will have cleaned and ironed a suitable altar cloth as discussed in a previous chapter. Spread it over your altar and begin to place your other tools on it. If you wish to have a picture, statue or symbolic representation of Isis, then place it in the center rear of the table. Before it, place the censer with the incense. To either side of the Goddess you may place your candles.

Your specially prepared salt should be placed next to the water dish on the left side of the altar and your magickal oil should be placed to the right. Place your beading tools right in front. *Everything that is to be placed on the altar should have been cleaned before you begin your ritual.*

Cleaning consists of:

1. Wash with water and your magickal salt.
2. Pass it through the smoke of some incense.
3. Anoint it with your magickal oil.

These actions will purify and prepare these objects to be powerful tools for the magick that you will be working.

**The Ritual Bath**

Before doing any sort of magick, it is traditional to prepare yourself with a physical and mental cleansing. This is done with a real bath, either a shower or tub bath, or even a sponging down if you are not able to take a full bath.

The ritual bath is a state of mind. If you are taking a tub bath, you should sprinkle some of the magickal salts you made into the tub along with several drops of the magickal oil. As you wash, be very conscious of clearing your mind of extraneous thoughts. Whatever worries you have, leave them outside the bathroom. (You can always come back to them later.) Think how wonderful it would be to set aside all unpleasant thoughts. Let your body rest from them. It is customary also not to think of the ritual you will soon be performing. Let your mind and body rest and cleanse.

Along with the physical dirt you're scrubbing off, visualize negativity washing off of you. See it come off in big ugly brownish-green streaks and neutralize in the holy water made from your magickal salts and oils.

If you are taking a shower, see the brownish-green goo washing down the drain. You can put a few drops of your magickal oil in the palm of your hand and rub it into your body. The warm shower will wash the excess oil off, and your skin will be left soft and magickally charged.

When your bath or shower is finished, anoint yourself with the magickal oil. To anoint, simply put a few drops in the palm of your hands, rub the hands together, then apply both hands to the directed area. After rubbing the area gently, keep the palms pressed to the area for a moment or two while you recite the words as follows:

Anoint your hands:

> *"May my hands work magick in harmony with my heart."*

Anoint your brow:

> *"May my concentration be true to bring my desire."*

Anoint your feet:

> *"May my feet ever tread on the path of honor and light."*

You are now ready to put on your robe, if you have one, and make your magick Love Charm.

*Part III*

# Chapter 9

## *The Ritual*

Symbolically seal yourself into your magickal room by closing the door. If it is possible to lock it, do so. The idea is that you will not emerge until your magick has been completed.

Light your candles and say:

> *"I declare this room a temple of light. I shall cleanse it to prepare the way to work my will."*

Mix three pinches of your magickal salt into your dish of water. Using the forefinger of your dominant hand,* stir the water and say:

> *"Let the sacred salt drive out all impurities from this water. May the light and love of Isis, Mistress of Magick, enter this water and make it holy."*

Beginning at the door to your temple and working in a general clockwise fashion, asperge (sprinkle the water) lightly throughout the perimeter of the room. Pay special attention to doors and windows. Work your way toward the altar—which should be the last item to be asperged.

Now light your incense, hold it aloft and say:

> *"May this sacrifice be pleasing to Isis. May*

---

* If you are right-handed, the dominant hand would be the right hand. If you are left-handed, this would be the left hand.

> these sacred herbs drive out all impurities
> within this temple to make it pleasing to the
> Goddess of Love."

Following the same pattern you used to aspurge your temple, now cense it. Take up the incense bowl and carry it around the edges of the room. End by thoroughly censing the altar.

When you have finished with the incense, replace it on your altar, hold your arms aloft to the heavens and declare:

> "I have made this temple pure for Isis, who is the fountain of all life. I have made this temple pure for Her holy presence. I have made this temple pure for Isis, Queen of all the Gods.
>
> "Oh Great Mother, I know something of the anguish and loneliness that you must have felt in the search for your lost husband, Osiris. I also know something of the joy you must have felt at finding him again. I too seek for love and ask that you be at my side to guard and guide me in my own quest.
>
> "Oh Great Mother, I also know something of the power of creation—the same power that you used to magickally restore life to Your husband. I too seek to work magick, to bring love into my life. I ask that you be at my side to lend me your power and wisdom—to guide me in this magickal quest.
>
> "I, (state your name), with the aid of Isis, the Supreme Mistress of Magick, call in the Powers of Light. I call in the Powers of Love. I ask that only that which is in my

*best interest be achieved.*

*"I now declare my purpose before all the Gods. May Anubis\* find me worthy and my heart pure!"*

At this point you may declare your personal magickal goal before the Gods. Tell Them what you wish to attain and why.

Example:

> *"Here, before Isis and the company of the Gods, I declare my purpose as a Quest of Love. I seek companionship, friendship and passionate love. I seek true happiness. The happiness that comes from sharing and stepping beyond my limitations. With the aid of the All Powerful Ones I cannot fail."*

Spend a moment preparing yourself for the work to come. Allow yourself to become as emotional as you can. Review the qualities that you want to attract. Review your desire for love. Allow

---

\* Anubis is the God who will weigh your heart (your intentions) on the day of your judgment to determine whether or not you are worthy of eternal life.

righteous anger to fill you—why have you been denied love? Why must you learn through pain? Demand joy and happiness! You deserve total happiness. If it seems appropriate, allow yourself to feel sexually aroused in your desire for love. Work up as much feeling and emotion as you can, and direct these feelings into your charm.

Now you may begin to make your Charm. Each bead that you pick up should be held for just a moment while you concentrate the power of your desire into it. Put the needle through the bead and remember that with each knot you make you are to lock your magickal formula (spell) into it. The formula should be whispered into the knot just as you tighten it. Keep your mind on what you are doing and do not let it wander.

When you have finished the Charm, sprinkle it with blessed water and pass it through the smoke of the incense. Raise it heavenward and say:

> "This Charm has been prepared according to ancient law and I have been true to my Higher Purpose. May Maat* judge the truth of my intentions, may Anubis find me pure of heart, and may Queen Isis have mercy on my needs and bring me total fulfillment of my heart's desire.
>
> "This Charm is strong. This Charm is pure of intent. This Charm is invincible according to sacred law. This Charm is sealed with the love and light of Isis. So be it."

The Charm does not have to be worn constantly, but it should be worn for at least 24 hours following this ritual, and then sleep with it under

---

* Maat is the Goddess of truth and justice.

your pillow for three consecutive nights.

To end the ritual, simply extinguish the candles and say:

> *"This rite has ended. The temple is now cleared."*

Any time you wish to recharge the Charm, simply repeat the chant on each bead. This is usually done before putting on the Charm. Just hold the necklace in your dominant hand and, using your thumb and forefinger, pause a moment on each bead to repeat your spell. You don't need to do this every time you want to wear the beads, but it is a good idea to do it every so often to keep them fully charged. The more you do it, the more energy they will hold.

To repeat what was said earlier: the knots of the necklace seal in the desire; the bead amplifies and charges the desire; so both knots and beads are important, working together. On completion, when the two ends are connected, it is like plugging into an energy source. The circuit is completed and fully charged. It creates its own energy field of attraction and amplifies your aura when you wear it. The more you wear the charm, the more powerful it becomes.

# Chapter 10

# *Dismantling Your Charm*

You may find that sometime in the future your Love Charm has been so effective you no longer have need of it and would prefer to use the beads for some other purpose. The following is a brief ritual that you may perform if, for any reason, you wish to dismantle your beads and discharge your magick.

Have your altar ready on which you should place a single white candle, a white flower, a dish of incense, an empty bowl (to catch the beads and string when the thread is cut) and a pair of sharp scissors. Light the candle and the incense, pick up the flower, and say the following:

> *"Holy Isis, Mother of Love, the path of life has led me onward and I find I am no longer in need of this magickal charm. I ask that the desires released from these knots be transformed into light and offered back to this planet for global healing."*

Place the flower at the base of the candle and, using the sharp scissors, proceed to cut through each knot on your charm, allowing the beads to fall into the bowl. Do not worry about the end knot if it is cemented with nail varnish. When you are finished say:

> "This magick has ended. May Isis guide my
> path."

Blow out the candle, allow the incense to burn out and offer the flower to the earth by going outside and placing it on the ground. (The flower has absorbed the energies of your magick charm and is transforming them into your wish for global healing.) Do not touch the flower once it has been offered back to the Earth.

The beads are now cleared and you may do with them as you wish.

## STAY IN TOUCH

On the following pages you will find listed, with their current prices, some of the books and tapes now available on related subjects. Your book dealer stocks most of these, and will stock new titles in the Llewellyn series as they become available. We urge your patronage.

To obtain a FREE COPY of our latest full CATALOG of New Age books, tapes, videos, crystals, products and services, just write to the address below. In each 80 page catalog sent out bimonthly, you will find articles, reviews, the latest information on New Age topics, a listing of news and events, and much more. It is an exciting and informative way to stay in touch with the New Age and the world. The first copy will be sent free of charge and you will continue receiving copies as long as you are an active customer. You may also subscribe to *The Llewellyn New Times* by sending a $2.00 donation ($7.00 for Canada & Mexico, and $20.00 for overseas). Order your copy of *The Llewellyn New Times* today!

*The Llewellyn New Times*
**P.O. Box 64383-Dept. 087, St. Paul, MN 55164**

## TO ORDER BOOKS AND PRODUCTS ON THE FOLLOWING PAGES:

If your book dealer does not carry the titles and products listed on the following pages, you may order them directly from Llewellyn. Just write us a letter. Please add $2 for postage and handling for orders of $10 and under. Orders over $10 require $3.50 postage and handling. (USA and in US funds). UPS Delivery: We ship UPS whenever possible. Delivery guaranteed. Provide your street address as UPS does not deliver to P.O. Boxes; UPS to Canada requires a $50 minimum order. Allow 4-6 weeks for delivery. Orders outside the USA and Canada: Airmail—add $5 per book; add $3 for each non-book item (tapes, etc.); add $1 per item for surface mail.

Send orders to:

**LLEWELLYN PUBLICATIONS**
**P.O. Box 64383-087**
**St. Paul, MN 55164-0383, U.S.A.**

## HOW TO DREAM YOUR LUCKY LOTTO NUMBERS
### By Raoul Maltagliati

Lotteries and sweepstakes are becoming increasingly popular, as people from many U.S. states wait hopefully for their chance at riches. Now Llewellyn introduces a book that no wishful lotto contestant could pass up.

*How to Dream your Lucky Lotto Numbers* is one of three exciting, mass-market how-to books coming this spring. Here Raoul Maltagliati tells:

* **How this system works**
* **How to discover the numeric value of various dream subjects**
* **How to interpret dreams**
* **And much more**

A comprehensive dream dictionary gives the meanings of various dreams, while letting the reader quickly find the numbers associated with a given dream.

The author also presents the underlying theory of dream analysis, information on the lotto, and an interview with an actual dream analyst who advises people on their lotto numbers.

**0-87542-483-X, mass market, illus.**                    **$3.95**

## HOW TO MAKE AND USE A MAGIC MIRROR
### by Donald Tyson

There's a "boy mechanic" at home in every one of us. As Henry Ford put the world on wheels, Donald Tyson is now opening New Worlds with simple psychic technology.

Author Donald Tyson takes the reader step-by-step through the creation of this powerful mystical tool. You will learn about:

* **Tools and supplies needed to create the mirror**
* **Construction techniques**
* **How to use the mirror for scrying (divination)**
* **How to communicate with spirits**
* **How to use the mirror for astral travel**

Tyson also presents a history of mirror lore in magic and literature. For anyone wanting their personal magical tool, *How to Make and Use a Magic Mirror* is a must item.

**0-87542-831-2, mass market, illus.**                    **$3.95**

## CHARMS, SPELLS AND FORMULAS
### by Ray Malbrough

In this book, Ray Malbrough reveals to you the secrets of Hoodoo magick. By using the simple materials available in Nature, you can bring about the necessary changes to greatly benefit your life and that of your friends. You are given detailed instructions for making and using the *gris-gris* (charm) bags only casually or mysteriously mentioned by other writers. Malbrough not only shows how to make gris-gris bags for health, money, luck, love and protection from evil and harm, etc., but he also explains how these charms work.

He also takes you into the world of *doll magick;* using dolls in rituals to gain love, success, or prosperity. Complete instructions are given for making the dolls and setting up the ritual.

Hoodoo magick can be as enjoyable as it is practical, and in this fascinating book you can learn how to be a *practitioner,* working your spells and charms for yourself or for others. Learn the methods which have been used successfully by Hoodoo practitioners for nearly 200 years, along with many practical tips for dealing with your clients.

0-87542-501-1, 192 pgs., 5¼ x 8, illus., softcover    $6.95

## THE COMPLETE BOOK OF INCENSE, OILS AND BREWS
### by Scott Cunningham

Scott Cunningham, world-famous expert on magical herbalism, first published *The Magic of Incense, Oils and Brews* in 1986. *The Complete Book of Incense, Oils and Brews* is a revised and expanded version of that book. Scott took readers' suggestions from the first edition and added more than 100 new formulas. Every page has been clarified and rewritten, and new chapters have been added.

There is no special, costly equipment to buy, and ingredients are usually easy to find. The book includes detailed information on a wide variety of herbs, sources for purchasing ingredients, substitutions for hard-to-find herbs, a glossary, and a chapter on creating your own magical recipes.

0-87542-128-8, 288 pgs., 5¼ x 8, illus., softcover   $12.95

## SECRETS OF GYPSY FORTUNETELLING
### by Raymond Buckland, Ph.D.

This book unveils the Romani secrets of fortune-telling, explaining in detail the many different methods used by these nomads. For generations they have survived on their skills as seers. Their accuracy is legendary. They are a people who seem to be born with "the sight" . . . the ability to look into the past, present and future using only the simplest of tools to aid them. Here you will learn to read palms, to interpret the symbols in a teacup, to read cards . . . both the Tarot and regular playing cards. Here are revealed the secrets of interpreting the actions of animals, of reading the weather, of recognizing birthmarks and the shape of hands. Impress your friends with your knowledge of many of these lesser Mysteries; uncommon forms of fortune-telling known only to a few.

**0-87542-051-6, mass market, 240 pgs., illus.**          **$3.95**

## TEA LEAF READING
### by William W. Hewitt

There may be more powerful methods of divination than tea leaf reading, but they also require heavy-duty commitment and disciplined training. Fun, lighthearted, and requiring very little discipline, tea leaf reading asks only of its practitioners an open mind and a spirit of adventure.

Just one cup of tea can give you a 12-month prophecy, or an answer to a specific question. It can also be used to examine the past. There is no regimen needed, no complicated rules to memorize. Simply read the instructions and look up the meanings of the symbols!

**0-87542-308-6, 240 pgs., mass market**          **$3.95**